Everyone Feels SAD Sometimes

by Marcie Aboff

illustrated by Damian Ward

PICTURE WINDOW BOOKS

a capstone imprint

Thanks to our adviser for his expertise, research, and advice:

Terry Flaherty, Ph.D., Professor of English
Minnesota State University, Mankato

Editors: Shelly Lyons and Jennifer Besel
Designer: Lori Bye
Art Director: Nathan Gassman
Production Specialist: Jane Klenk

The illustrations in this book were created digitally.

Picture Window Books
151 Good Counsel Drive
P.O. Box 669
Mankato, MN 56002-0669
877-845-8392
www.picturewindowbooks.com

Printed in the United States of America in North Mankato, Minnesota.
092009
005618CGS10

 All books published by Picture Window Books
are manufactured with paper containing at least
10 percent post-consumer waste.

Library of Congress Cataloging-in-Publication Data
Aboff, Marcie.
Everyone feels sad sometimes / by Marcie Aboff ; illustrated by Damian Ward.
p. cm. – (Everyone has feelings)
Includes index.
ISBN 978-1-4048-5755-1 (library binding)
ISBN 978-1-4048-6114-5 (paperback)
1. Sadness–Juvenile literature. 2. Sadness in children–Juvenile literature.
I. Ward, Damian, 1977- II. Title.
BF723.S15A38 2010
152.4–dc22
2009024064

Everyone has feelings. Sometimes people feel happy. Other times people feel sad. People can feel angry or scared, too. These feelings are normal.

HAPPY

SAD

ANGRY

SCARED

There are many ways of showing sadness. There are many ways to feel less sadness, too.

Jack's soccer game was canceled because of a storm.
Jack's heart feels heavy.

Jack's mom tells him to think about playing the game. Jack draws a picture of a soccer game.

Zack watches the other kids play kickball.
Some of the kids told him he couldn't play.

Zack looks at the ground.
His throat feels tight.

Zack talks to the kids. They let him play.

Soon he's having a blast!

Cory gets a bad grade on his spelling test.

animal
xbaloon
xmonckee
who
hild

His eyes start to burn. His lips start to shake. He puts his head down on his desk.

Cory tells his dad about the test. His dad helps him study the spelling words.

Angie's best friend, Sara, is moving away. Angie wants Sara to stay.

Angie's face feels hot. Tears roll down her face.

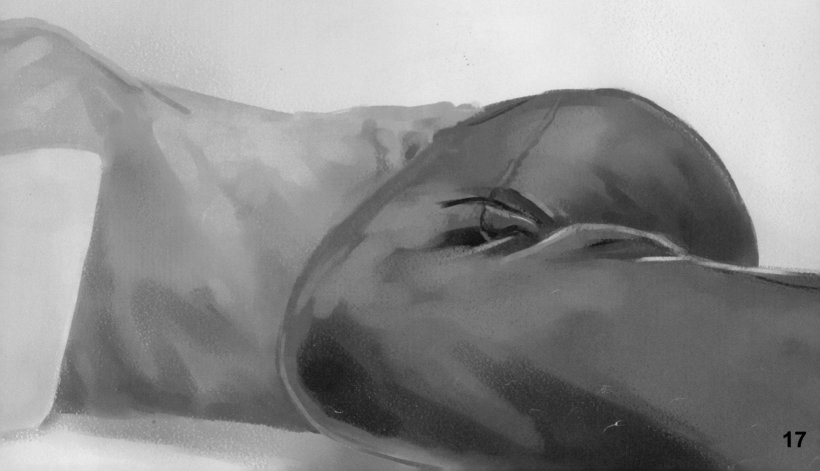

Angie talks to her mom about her feelings. Angie calls Sara on the phone.

They make plans to see each other during summer vacation.

Rachel's dog, Buddy, is sick. Rachel starts to cry. She wants him to feel better.

Rachel's dad takes
Buddy to the vet.

Rachel's mom gives her a hug. Rachel
thinks about her dog getting well.

Things to do when you feel sad:

- Talk to an adult about your feelings.
- Cry until you feel better.
- Ask a parent for a hug.
- Think about something that makes you happy.
- Play with your favorite toy.
- Draw a picture that makes you smile.

Glossary

feelings—emotions; anger, sadness, and happiness are all kinds of feelings.

sadness—an unhappy or troubled feeling

vacation—a time spent away from home or school

More Books to Read

Medina, Sarah. *Sad*. Chicago: Heinemann Library, 2007.

Moroney, Tracey. *When I'm Feeling Sad*. Columbus, Ohio: Gingham Dog Press, 2006.

Snow, Todd, and Peggy Snow. *Feelings to Share from A to Z*. Oak Park Heights, Minn.: Maren Green Pub., 2007.

Verroken, Sarah. *Feeling Sad*. Brooklyn, N.Y.: Enchanted Lion Books, 2009.

Internet Sites

FactHound offers a safe, fun way to find Internet sites related to this book. All of the sites on FactHound have been researched by our staff.

Here's all you do:

Visit *www.facthound.com*

FactHound will fetch the best sites for you!

Look for all of the books in the Everyone Feels series:

Everyone Feels Angry Sometimes

Everyone Feels Happy Sometimes

Everyone Feels Sad Sometimes

Everyone Feels Scared Sometimes